IN THE CARE OF EVIL:
THE DISAPPEARANCE AND DEATH OF MARGARET FLEMING

Dr. Hilary A. Nettleton

Grosvenor House
Publishing Limited

All rights reserved
Copyright © Dr Hilary A Nettleton, 2020

The right of Dr Hilary A Nettleton to be
identified as the author of this
work has been asserted in accordance with Section 78
of the Copyright, Designs and Patents Act 1988

The book cover is copyright to Dr Hilary A Nettleton

This book is published by
Grosvenor House Publishing Ltd
Link House
140 The Broadway, Tolworth, Surrey, KT6 7HT.
www.grosvenorhousepublishing.co.uk

This book is sold subject to the conditions that it shall not, by way of
trade or otherwise, be lent, resold, hired out or otherwise circulated
without the author's or publisher's prior consent in any form of binding or
cover other than that in which it is published and
without a similar condition including this condition being imposed
on the subsequent purchaser.

A CIP record for this book
is available from the British Library

ISBN 978-1-83975-161-5

AUTHOR BACKGROUND

Dr Hilary A Nettleton is a criminologist with extensive experience teaching and researching in criminology and criminal justice. She holds a PhD in Criminology from the University of Bristol as well an M.A, MPhil in Criminology from Keele University. She has previously worked for the Scottish Office (Criminology Research Unit) as well as the Home Office and the Institute of Psychiatry in South London. Hilary has worked in maximum-security prisons throughout the UK, interviewing Category A long-term prisoners who have been convicted of the most serious offences. She has also worked as a research fellow, evaluating police initiatives around tackling alcohol related violent crime. Her most recent position is as an associate lecturer in criminology at the Open University.

Hilary published her first true crime book entitled *The Cruellest Con* (Grosvenor House Publishing) in January 2020.

Introduction

Chapter 1	Margaret's Early Life in Port Glasgow and Key Turning Points	1
Chapter 2	Cairney and Jones Take Control of Margaret: A Life of Misery at 'Seacroft'	10
Chapter 3	Suspicions, Fantastical Tales & The Police Investigation Begins	26
Chapter 4	No Body: No Case? The Police Investigation Intensifies	43
Chapter 5	The Net Closes In: The Case Goes to Trial at Glasgow High Court	53
Chapter 6	The Day of Judgement: Sentencing at the High Court	73
Chapter 7	Lessons Learnt and Caring for Vulnerable People: How Unique is the Margaret Fleming Case?	77
Chapter 8	Discussion and Conclusion	84

INTRODUCTION

In 2016 a crime so heinous hit the national media, that it outraged and shocked all who heard and read about it. Many questioned how such a crime could take place in modern Britain. The case centred on the mysterious disappearance of a, then 36-year-old woman, called Margaret Fleming, from a house set on the banks of the River Clyde in Scotland.

Prior to her disappearance, Margaret, who had learning difficulties, had lived with her carers, Edward (Eddie) Cairns and Avril Jones, in their dilapidated waterfront property, 'Seacroft', in Inverkip, Inverclyde. At first sight 'Seacroft' seems like an idyllic house to grow up in. The house enjoys stunning views across the Firth of Clyde and is located on the outskirts of the quiet village of Inverkip. However, this home was anything but a peaceful sanctuary. Instead, in 2016 it became the centre of one of Scotland's most horrifying murder trials.

As more information emerged, it was discovered that there had been no independent sighting of Margaret Fleming at 'Seacroft', or anywhere else for that matter, in almost two decades. The reality was that none of her friends, neighbours or family members had actually seen her in a considerable number of years. In fact, she was only 19 years old when she was last seen by anyone *other than* Cairney and Jones. It was not until October 2016, following a missed appointment for a benefits review, that police and social services began an official investigation into Margaret's disappearance.

The long police investigation that followed showed the lengths that two killers were prepared to go to in order to hide their cruel and evil actions against a defenceless young woman. The investigation also showed how easy it was for a vulnerable woman to completely vanish without anyone apparently taking notice of the fact that she was missing. The fact that Margaret disappeared for so long with little or no concern for her well-being is surely a damning indictment of the official systems and support structures around fragile individuals like Margaret. Not one person reported her missing. However, nothing should overshadow the complete culpability of Cairney and Jones in carrying out such a heinous crime. For almost two decades the pair hid their crime and concocted a litany of fantastical stories about where Margaret was – all the time insisting that she was still alive and well.

This book charts many of the complexities that surrounded Margaret Fleming's disappearance. In particular, it examines the investigation carried out by Police Scotland and the evidence that culminated in Cairney and Jones' arrest in October 2017. The book also examines the key reasons why her two killers were successfully convicted of her murder in the absence of Margaret's body. At the time of writing (2020) no trace of Margaret

Fleming has ever been found, despite extensive police searches of the area.

It is important to note at this point that, while Margaret's early life (up to the point at which she went to live with Cairney and Jones) is well documented, the harrowing details of her life with Cairney and Jones only became public knowledge during the seven-week trial of her two killers at Glasgow High Court.

This book is respectfully dedicated to the memory of Margaret Fleming. May she rest in peace and know that she was loved.

Chapter 1

Margaret's Early Life in Port Glasgow and Key Turning Points

Margaret Fleming was born on the 1 November 1980 and grew up in a relatively comfortable middle-class household in the town of Port Glasgow in Scotland. Port Glasgow is the second largest town in the Inverclyde Council area and has a population of approximately 15,000. It is a former shipbuilding town located on the banks of the River Clyde and it is situated 18 miles from the urban sprawl of the city of Glasgow.

Margaret grew up as an only child and was adored by her parents and wider family. Her father, Derek Fleming, was a tradesman who retrained as a lawyer and her mother, Margaret Cruickshanks, was a stay-at-home mum. By all accounts, Margaret experienced a number of challenges very early on in her life. Many of the problems that she faced as a child centred on the fact that she had moderate learning difficulties. This meant that she struggled with basic literacy and numeracy and so needed additional support. Despite living with these difficulties from a young age, Margaret attended a mainstream primary school in Port Glasgow (Slaemuir Primary) where she received help with basic reading and writing. Margaret's learning difficulties did not stop her making friends, however, and she was well liked by the teachers and pupils alike.

Since her case appeared in the national newspapers, many of Margaret's old school friends have spoken out about what she was like at school. These recollections paint a picture of a young woman who was extremely kind, well-meaning and most happy when she was listening to music. Speaking to the *Glasgow Times* newspaper in 2019, Margaret's old classmate, Lynn Foreman, said:

"As Slaemuir Primary was such a small school we all helped her out. We were like a family and everyone can remember her. I remember Margaret; she was lovely, she didn't have any badness in her and she was really kind. She was happy if everyone else was happy, she looked out for other people, she was such a caring girl and so gentle. My mum used to be a parent helper and she used to love it if Margaret was in her group as she was lovely and never caused her any bother. Her gran and grandad just adored her."

Similarly, old school friend Gillian Sherrard McCulloch recalled that:

"Everybody was pals with Margaret and we all looked out for her at school. Margaret was a lovely girl who so many of us thought about over the years – we never forgot Margaret."

Margaret Fleming at Primary School in Port Glasgow:
Credit the Greenock Telegraph

Former classmate Jon Cox, who was also in Margaret's primary school class, said:

"I was quite close to her at school and actually invited her to the P7 school dance. I remember her dad picking us up and Margaret's mum was crying because she was overwhelmed that someone had invited her daughter to the dance. Margaret was pure love; there was no malice or hate in her. For those who know the book Of Mice and Men, *Margaret was a bit like Lennie. She was a lovely human being, very quiet and timid even to the people who knew her. She always gave you a big heartfelt smile – she was a beautiful person."*

Once Margaret left primary school in Port Glasgow and moved up to Port Glasgow High School, she continued to be popular and to require additional learning support.

When Margaret's old English teacher, Jackie Cahill, attended court in 2019 (during the court case over Margaret's disappearance) she talked about Margaret's difficulties at school:

"She struggled to put pen to paper. She struggled to read and read at about the level of an eight-year-old."

Margaret also required additional support to motivate her to work. In a report written by Margaret's schoolteacher, Elizabeth Brown (in 1995), she recalled that:

"If you left Margaret on her own she would do very little. You had to prod her to do the work. Her marks were all at the very bottom end of the school."

Retired teacher, Elaine Moore, also observed that Margaret was:

"Quite isolated. Her and her dad were a wee unit. She was concerned about him and he was concerned about her."

All of the above recollections support the picture of Margaret Fleming as a very popular girl with both her friends and teachers. While there can be no doubt that she struggled with learning throughout her schooling, this did not impede her making friends and being sociable and well liked by others.

While Margaret's early life in Port Glasgow was undoubtedly a happy and relatively carefree one, two significant events took place later on in her teenage years that altered the course of her life and ultimately put her into the hands of her killers.

The first life-changing event was the divorce of her parents. In January 1993, Margaret's parents, Derek and Margaret, made the decision to divorce after 20 years together. As with most teenagers, the end of her parents' marriage caused Margaret massive personal torment and upheaval. She was also an only child and so did not have the support from any brothers or sisters. Once the divorce of her parents was finalised, Margaret left the family home with her dad and they both went to live with her paternal grandparents (Fergie and Nora). By all accounts, Margaret was extremely close to her dad and relied on him for support and guidance. It is

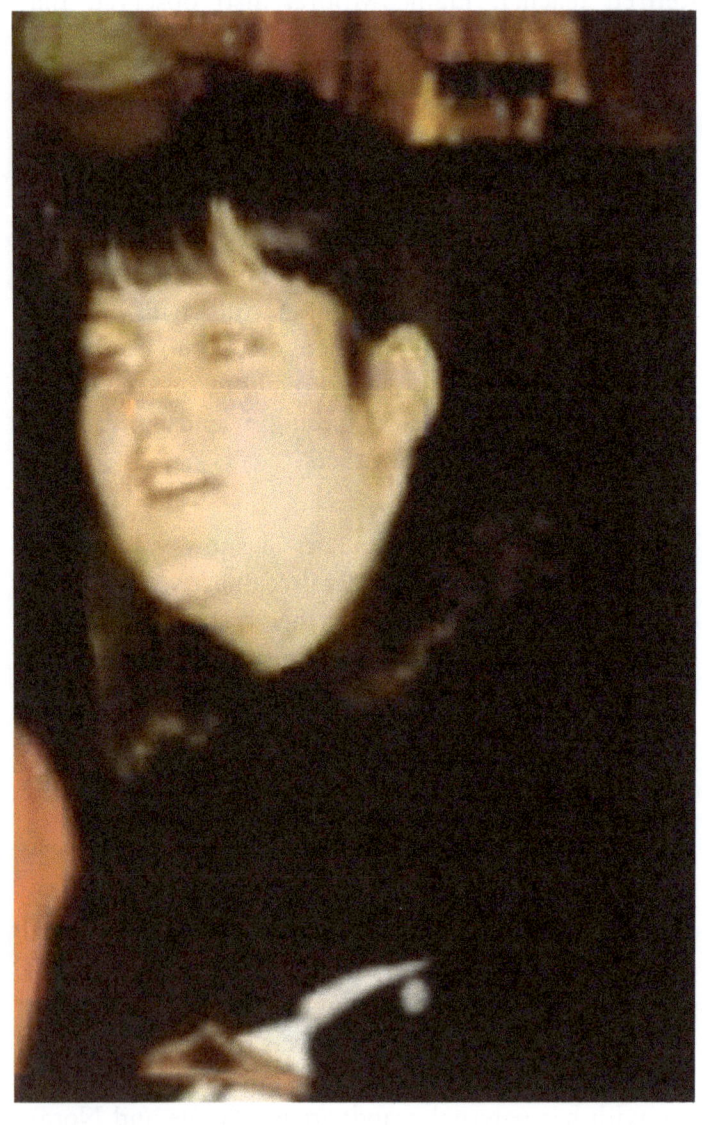

Margaret pictured as a teenager: Credit the Greenock Telegraph

clear from research, however, that Margaret's parents and grandparents all struggled to look after her and found her behaviour sometimes too difficult to handle. In particular, there seems to have been a lot of tension existing between Margaret and her mum.

The second important turning point in Margaret Fleming's life was the death of her father in October 1995. Margaret's dad, Derek Fleming, had been diagnosed with terminal cancer but was so protective of his young daughter that he hid from her how ill he actually was and the reasons why he had to go to hospital so often. While her dad was in hospital, Margaret would often stay with her grandparents. Given that father and daughter were so close, Derek Fleming's death was an enormous shock to Margaret and it caused great upheaval in her young life. Margaret's father undoubtedly represented stability to the teenager and losing him would, no doubt, have completely shaken her world.

The divorce of her parents, quickly followed by the death of her beloved father only two years later, seems to have led to a downward spiral in Margaret's behaviour. Margaret was clearly upset and angry for some time after her dad died and acted out her frustrations while living with her grandparents and mother while her father's estate was settled. At this time, Margaret's behaviour declined so much that her mother arranged a meeting with social workers at Inverclyde Council Social Work Department to discuss getting some support from the Additional Needs Team there. In this meeting and according to records, a social worker observed that Margaret was *'a naïve girl; quite vulnerable, quiet,*

DR. HILARY A. NETTLETON

Margaret in happier times holding a small child:
Credit the Greenock Telegraph

lonely, sad'. The social worker also noted an obviously strained relationship between mother and daughter. Giving evidence in court in 2019, she said:

"When I went to their house to pick up Margaret, I would have a conversation with her mum who found it difficult. She had lived on her own and now had an adolescent girl who was missing her dad."

The social worker continued to support Margaret Fleming until she went on maternity leave in July 1996. By the following month, Margaret's mother informed the Social Work Department that her daughter's behaviour had continued to deteriorate. Margaret Cruickshanks claimed that she received no further support and no one stepped in to replace the role of Margaret's allocated social worker.

Unfortunately, however, things were only to get much worse once Edward Cairney and Avril Jones entered the picture. Margaret Fleming was only a teenager when she moved in with the couple that would cause her untold misery and ultimately end her life.

Chapter 2

Cairney and Jones Take Control of Margaret: A Life of Misery at 'Seacroft'

As Margaret Fleming's behaviour became more difficult to deal with following her dad's death, the insidious presence of Edward Cairney and Avril Jones began to take hold.

Whether, initially at least, Cairney and Jones harboured some altruistic motive towards Margaret Fleming – namely that they wanted to help out Margaret's mother in her time of distress following the death of her ex-husband and the father of her daughter – seems highly unlikely. A more realistic interpretation is that from the outset, Cairney and Jones planned all along to take advantage of the Fleming family. The pair knew that in addition to claiming a number of social security benefits, Margaret Fleming had also been left some money by both her dad and his parents. But who were the rather odd couple?

IN THE CARE OF EVIL

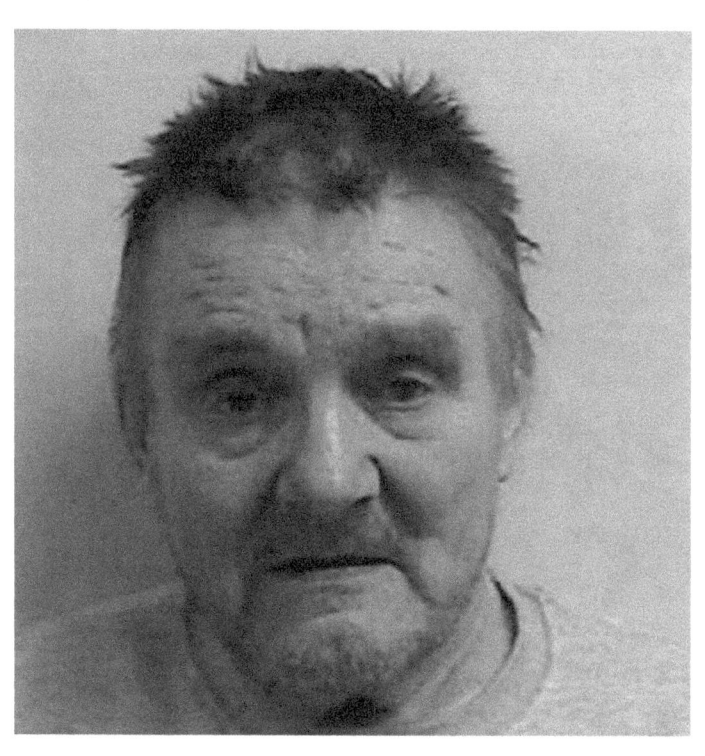

Edward Cairney's police photo taken following his arrest:
Credit the Greenock Telegraph

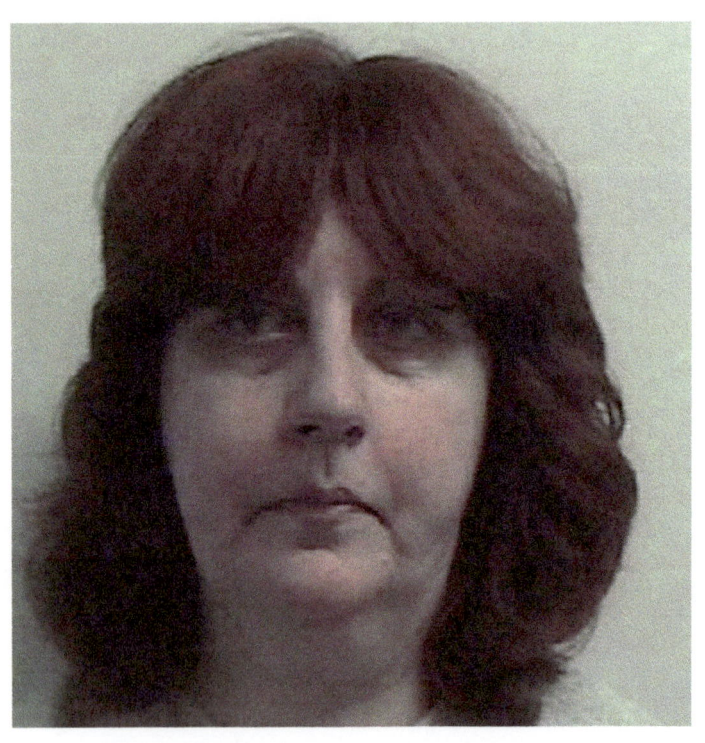

The police photo of Avril Jones taken after her arrest:
Credit the Greenock Telegraph

At the time of Derek Fleming's death in 1995, Edward Cairney was 52 years old and a one-time bare-knuckle boxer and deep-sea diver who bragged about his supposed connections to the notorious Kray twins in London. Despite being physically strong in his younger years age had taken its toll on Cairney and in his later years he resorted to the use of sticks and a wheelchair due to a back injury. Personality-wise Edward Cairney was a loud, bombastic individual who was forceful in expressing his opinions. Cairney's long-term companion, Avril Jones, was reserved and quiet by comparison. She had previously been employed as a legal secretary and had also helped Cairney run a local hotel in Port Glasgow. In 1995, Jones was 34 years old and often deferred to the much older and more confident Cairney. The precise nature of the relationship between the pair has never been fully established (they did intonate to reporter Russell Findley in 2017 that it was 'business based' rather than 'romantic') but it is clear that both were equally complicit in hatching the plot to get rid of Margaret and keep claiming her benefits money. A key question is why Cairney and Jones, with little apparent experience of looking after young adults with behavioural problems, ended up as Margaret's sole carers at their dilapidated property in Inverkip.

Ironically the key to their sole guardianship lies with Margaret's own father Derek. While it is not clear how long Derek Fleming knew the pair or in what context they met initially, Derek Fleming undoubtedly considered Cairney and Jones, friends. So much so that he had made a stipulation in his will that, in the event of his death, his daughter was to be looked after by them. It is a truly tragic irony that Mr Fleming was so concerned about his daughter's future that he believed that she would be safer living with his friends – friends who would eventually go on to kill his daughter.

Cairney and Jones were also considered close enough friends to Derek Fleming that, after his death, they helped to arrange his funeral. This fact is supported by Jean McSherry, Mr Fleming's fiancée prior to his death in October 1995. She revealed the contents of a brief note written by both Margaret Fleming and her father's parents in which they expressed *'special thanks'* to 'Eddie' and Avril for arranging Derek's funeral.

During the High Court trial, Margaret Fleming's mother (Margaret Cruickshanks) revealed that she only met Cairney and Jones for the first time at Derek's funeral.

She said:

"After Derek died, they (Cairney and Jones) were at the funeral. Eddie Cairney came and approached me and said that if I needed any help with Margaret, he would give me respite care."

The court heard that Margaret initially lived with her mother but later spent up to a fortnight at a time living with Cairney and Jones at their run down house in Inverkip. By the age of 17, however, Margaret was living with the couple on a full-time basis.

There can be no doubt that between the death of Derek Fleming in October 1995 and August 1996, when her mother contacted Inverclyde Social Services Department to inform them that her daughter's behaviour was too difficult for her to deal with on her own, Edward Cairney and Avril Jones had formulated their plan to take over control of Margaret Fleming. Cairney in particular, did this by making sure that Margaret was isolated from her family and that he and Jones were the sole 'gatekeepers' to Margaret's money. The physical location of 'Seacroft' suited this purpose – situated as it was on the Clyde Coast, 10 miles away from Margaret's family in Port Glasgow. The location of 'Seacroft' was remote enough to ensure that it would be difficult for any of Margaret's friends and family to just 'pop in' to see her.

Jean McSherry, Derek Fleming's fiancée prior to his death, claimed that she tried to speak to Margaret after she began living with the pair in Inverkip but was always denied contact by Cairney and Jones. Giving evidence in court Ms McSherry recalled that:

"They told me that she was nothing to do with me… Eddie spoke to me on the phone, when he said 'no' he meant 'no'."

Importantly, Cairney and Jones also made sure that Margaret Fleming's own mother had no contact with her daughter. In November 1997 Margaret's ties with her mother were finally severed after Cairney assaulted Ms Cruickshanks when she went to 'Seacroft'. Margaret Cruickshanks alleges that she went to Inverkip to tell the couple that she wanted to bring her daughter back home. She recalls that Cairney brought her daughter downstairs from her attic bedroom and asked her where she wanted to live. Clearly frightened of the couple and under pressure to comply, Margaret Fleming told her mum that she wanted to stay with Cairney and Jones in Inverkip. Unsurprisingly, Cairney (speaking later in court during his High Court trial) had a very different interpretation of the same meeting. He firmly blamed Margaret's mother for what had happened that day:

"Her mother was slavering, shrieking at me and stamping her feet. Wee Margaret got alarmed at this and ran in and put her arms round me. That was the last straw. Her mother charged out the door. It's easy to see where the wean got her lunacy from."

Margaret's mother later recalled that, following this visit in 1997 she contacted the police who went to check up on Margaret's welfare. She recalled that the police:

"came back to me to say that she was all right. As far as I knew that was where she was living. I didn't visit anymore. I then got a letter. It said that she didn't want to see me anymore."

In the months that followed, one can only imagine that, firmly separated from her mother and friends, the teenage Margaret Fleming became increasingly isolated and controlled by the two people who were meant to be 'caring' for her. On 21 October 1999, records confirm that Margaret saw her GP, Dr James Farrell, at Port Glasgow Health Centre for the last time. Speaking in court (in 2019) Dr Farrell reiterated that Margaret had *'quite significant learning difficulties'* and, in his opinion, believed that she may have had SOTOS syndrome from birth but a definitive diagnosis was never made. SOTOS syndrome is a genetic disorder affecting children that can lead to learning disabilities and behavioural problems. Dr Farrell also noted at the time, that she was *'socially and educationally isolated'* and referred her to the Renfrewshire and Inverclyde Community Learning Disability Team. Psychologist Dr Alan Smith from the team interviewed Margaret, as well as Cairney and Jones, at their home in Inverkip before Christmas 1999. Dr Smith scheduled a follow-up appointment but this was cancelled by Avril Jones.

In police statements, Avril Jones's own mother (Florence Jones) recalled last seeing Margaret in March 1999. She remembers Margaret as a *'very, very quiet girl who 'couldn't look after herself due to her learning difficulties'*. She confirmed that Margaret was present at her ruby wedding celebrations in March 1999.

The last confirmed sighting of Margaret came from Richard Jones, the brother of Avril Jones, on 17 December 1999. He vividly remembers the then 19-year-old Margaret coming to his new house in Inverkip and playing with his two children in the garden. Crucially, Richard Jones also recalls that when the family met the following week for Christmas dinner, Margaret was not there. This is also confirmed in photographs taken at that time where Margaret is not present in any of them.

There can be little doubt that once isolated at 'Seacroft', life for Margaret Fleming was an untold nightmare. Cairney and Jones were in deep financial straits, thousands of pounds in arrears on their mortgage, and so saw Margaret as an easy solution to their money problems. Sadly, it was Margaret Fleming who paid the

DR. HILARY A. NETTLETON

The last known picture of Margaret Fleming taken with relatives at a family celebration in Inverkip: Credit the Greenock Telegraph

ultimate price for their greed and cruelty. There is little doubt that, with little or no contact with the outside world, 'Seacroft' became Margaret's prison for the last two years of her life.

If the condition of the house in 2016 was anything to go by, Margaret lived her last days in a filthy house that was in a state of serious disrepair. 'Seacroft' was squalid and generally unfit for human habitation. According to police, the kitchen was littered with rotting food and overflowing bin bags. Hair and even faeces from the couple's two dogs also lay inside the home. Furniture and junk was piled high to the ceiling. Decaying refuse had even been stuffed beneath the floorboards. All of this gave the impression of Cairney and Jones as unable to look after themselves, never mind a fragile and vulnerable young women like Margaret Fleming.

The appalling condition of 'Seacroft' was matched only by the appalling treatment handed out to Margaret while she lived there. Evidence given at the 2019 trial confirmed that Margaret was subjected to horrific treatment from the couple. Reports are that she was forced to endure 'punishments' from Cairney and Jones on a daily basis. These included being tied up regularly, having her hair hacked short, and being deprived of food. Her last days at 'Seacroft' must have been a living hell. Giving evidence at the High Court, Police Scotland spoke to witnesses who:

"... would tell us that they would find her with her arms taped up, locked in bedrooms, kids invited in to play because they knew that would really upset Margaret. In

The dilapidated condition of 'Seacroft' is evident in this photograph. Edward Cairney is pictured walking around in the garden of the property: Credit the Greenock Telegraph

This photo clearly shows 'Seacroft' in a clear state of serious disrepair:
Credit: the Greenock Telegraph

"Seacroft Cottage" in Inverkip, Renfrewshire:
Credit: the Greenock Telegraph

IN THE CARE OF EVIL

Seacroft photographed from the main road in Inverkip:
Credit the Greenock Telegraph

Seacroft enjoyed stunning views from the back garden over the Firth of Clyde: Credit the Greenock Telegraph

effect they tortured her. Her hands were being bound and she was not allowed to sit at the table when people were invited round for dinner. It reminded me of someone being treated as a slave."

Although visitors to the house were rare; those who did visit describe seeing Margaret bound by gaffer tape and locked in her bedroom with plastic tubes on her arms. They were told that this was done in order to stop Margaret self-harming. The brother of Avril Jones, Richard Jones, recalled arriving at 'Seacroft' in April 1999 (the day after his parents' wedding anniversary) to discover that Margaret was locked in her bedroom with plastic tubes on her arms. He then recalls hearing Margaret making a chilling wailing sound while scraping her nails down the window.

The treatment imposed upon Margaret Fleming by her two killers was clearly cruel and extensive. She was a high risk young woman who should have been looked after and supported by the two people whose care she was entrusted into. Cairney and Jones however, abused that trust in the worst way possible when they tortured Margaret, stole from her, and ultimately ended her life. And yet over nearly two decades, none of Margaret's friends or family members noticed that she was absent or reported her missing to the police. As the years passed by with no repercussions from the authorities, Margaret's two killers undoubtedly became more confident that their crimes would never be exposed. However, that was all about to change in 2016 when a change to the benefits system set in motion a series of events that shone a very bright light on Margaret's life at 'Seacroft'.

Chapter 3

Suspicions, Fantastical Tales & The Police Investigation Begins

Concerns about Margaret Fleming's well-being were not raised by a worried family member, neighbour or friend but following formal changes made to the benefits system in 2016. It is arguable that had these changes not been made when they were, Margaret's benefits would continue to have been paid unchallenged into Avril Jones's bank account and the evil actions of the couple gone undiscovered.

In 2016, the key benefit change involved replacing Disability Living Allowance (DLA) with Personal Independence Payments (PIP). Recipients of DLA would now only be able to move to PIP following a new claim application and, crucially, a face-to-face assessment of their eligibility. As she had done for a number of years, it was Avril Jones who completed the new benefits claim on Margaret's behalf. However, Margaret herself was required to attend an assessment with the health firm 'Atos' in Glasgow on the 27th of October 2016 to assess the extent of her disabilities. Jones later claimed during her trial that Margaret was adamant that she would not go to this assessment:

"She had an appointment for PIP but I knew she wouldn't go. She was petrified of authority. We were going out the door and I said 'Right, you ready?' She pushed me, down I went, and she shot out the door, saying 'I'm not going'."

The sad truth of the matter, however, was that this was all lies. Margaret could not have attended the assessment because she was not alive at this point and had not been so for a considerable number of years.

A positive outcome of Margaret's non-attendance in Glasgow was that it set in motion a number of safety alerts. The 'Atos' nurse due to have assessed Margaret telephoned Avril Jones on the same day to find out why Margaret had not attended her session. The nurse was unhappy with the response(s) given by Jones and went on to raise her concern with social workers at Inverclyde Council. At the same time, the Department of Work and Pensions also seemed to be raising their own doubts about some of the claims made by Jones on the PIP form that she had completed on Margaret's behalf. The claims were deemed unusual because they did not seem to match what the authorities already knew about the then 36-year-old Margaret's health.

In the application for PIP, Avril Jones wrote the following (the claims are worth repeating here because of the importance of the response they triggered):

'Margaret needs constant care. She self-harms and needs daily checks to see that her body has no new wounds. She point-blank refuses to go to her doctor as this will lead to an asylum. Margaret does not have a proper understanding of hygiene. Her period time is a nightmare. She needs to be told when to change because I can smell her. She cannot be trusted with food since it was discovered that she was caught eating out of the dog's bowl of scraps. Margaret has also made jam sandwiches whilst on her period, wiping 'mess' onto bread! She is never alone for her own and others' safety. If she got lost around lots of people she would panic. If anyone were to offer to help her, she'd go with them. In that sense she does not see the danger and never will.'

These claims were clearly extreme and, if true, presented Margaret as a woman at great risk. When the form was received, a social worker phoned Avril Jones to offer help and was told that Margaret had *'picked a hole in her head but refused to see a doctor'*.

Importantly, the claims made by Avril Jones raised the suspicions of a social worker at Inverclyde Council who then alerted the police. On 28 October 2016, Sgt Chris McKay of Police Scotland responded to these concerns and, following an initial visit to 'Seacroft', launched a 'missing persons inquiry'.

From the outset, Cairney and Jones were remarkable for their lack of concern about Margaret's welfare. They simply seemed unmoved by the plight of the vulnerable young woman entrusted into their care since the mid-1990s. The pair claimed that there was nothing to be concerned about because Margaret was still alive but just had a habit of running away. Cairney even made the claim that Margaret was 'very cunning' and would often taunt him about running away and getting him charged with murder.

Cairney even told police that when they first visited 'Seacroft', Margaret was actually in the house. He stated that he and Margaret had just returned (by bus) from a shopping trip to the nearby town of Wemyss Bay. They both entered the house through the back door and Cairney claims that he then went into the hallway leaving Margaret 'hovering' in the kitchen. However, Margaret fled out of the back door when she heard police officers at the door. Cairney claimed that Margaret was frightened of authority figures because she feared being taken into care. Cairney even criticised the police for not looking more widely for Margaret on that night, insisting that she had left 'Seacroft' on foot and so could not be far away.

Cairney said:

"I told them, 'That's the way she had to go, if you move quickly you'll get her.' She went through them. They must have seen her."

Under police questioning, Cairney and Jones continued to be evasive. They stuck to their story that Margaret was still alive but was in the habit of running away. The pair claimed that when she ran off, she would often not tell them where she was going. When they did ask who she was going to spend time with, she would say 'that's private'. Between 1999 and 2016, the couple were vague about how often Margaret visited and how long she stayed for. In fact, they offered little evidence that she was ever at the house. Speaking of Margaret, Cairney later said that:

"After she turned 17 I've got no idea of how long or where we saw her. She came here for money; it was always money. That's the only reason she came back."

The pair portrayed her as an unruly teenager who defied their rules and came and went as she pleased.

Revealingly when Cairney and Jones' neighbours were questioned by the police, they said that they were under the impression that it was only the Eddie and Avril who lived in the house. Many had no recollection at all of a young woman fitting Margaret's description coming or going from 'Seacroft'. Even Avril Jones's own niece (Shannon Jones), who stayed at the house for six months in 2007, stated that she never saw Margaret Fleming in the house the whole time that she was there.

One of Cairney and Jones' most repeated stories was that Margaret disappeared in order to visit the Millennium Dome in London after it opened in 2000. Cairney told police that Margaret was fascinated with the attraction and had defiantly run off when she was told that she could not go:

"We told Margaret that she couldn't keep disappearing because it was a worry. She would need to stop it but she took off again."

To support his story, Cairney claimed that Margaret had sent them letters from her first two trips there. These letters were relatively well written and suspicions were immediately raised that they could be the work of a young woman who struggled to read and write. In 2019 the authenticity of these letters formed a crucial part of the Crown's case against Cairney and Jones.

While police initially began their investigation in October 2016 as a 'missing persons inquiry', the investigation team soon realized after months of enquiries, that all was not well at 'Seacroft' and that something more sinister could have happened to Margaret. This conclusion was reached, not only because of the outlandish stories told by Cairney and Jones about Margaret's lifestyle but because of the lack of information that existed about her. There was simply little evidence of her being alive.

As part of the police 'proof of life' investigation – the process whereby police check the records of every health board, hospital, doctor's surgery, police force and local authority to look for signs of activity – police travelled all across the UK to follow up leads about where Margaret might be. Leads were also followed up with Margaret's extended family in the USA and efforts were made to rule out the identity of every other 'Margaret Fleming' living in the UK. Banks and lending institutions were also contacted to see if Margaret had made any recent applications for credit. After an exhaustive 13-month search no new information about Margaret was obtained.

Officers also sifted through thousands of items of paperwork, documents and articles taken from 'Seacroft', and got in touch with over 1,200 individuals and organisations who may have had contact with Ms Fleming. Of the 1000 statements taken by the police, the majority reported not having seen Margaret in a considerable number of years. As previously mentioned, neighbours of Cairney and Jones who provided witness statements to the police, believed that the couple lived alone at 'Seacroft' because they only saw either Cairney or Jones arriving or leaving the house.

Crucial to finding evidence that something sinister might have happened to Margaret, was the forensic search of the inside of 'Seacroft'. On first visiting 'Seacroft' on 28 October 2016, police had to fight their way through piles of junk just to get into the house. Four days later, officers began their detailed forensic search of the property. This search was thorough and involved clearing the inside of the house out one room at a time and then spraying luminol throughout each room in order to detect any traces of blood which might indicate that Margaret had been assaulted in some way inside the property. Luminol is a powerful chemical that can detect the smallest amounts of blood at crime scenes. No traces of blood were ever discovered during the examination at 'Seacroft'.

What seemed remarkable about the inside of the property was that there was simply no trace of Margaret living there; no personal items like make-up, a toothbrush or hairbrush that might have indicated that she actually lived there. When police first attended

'Seacroft', the attic room that Margaret allegedly slept in had no bed or carpet in it and was cluttered with a 3 feet mountain of rubbish. Of the thousands of photographs seized from the house, very few were of Margaret. Even in diaries seized belonging to Avril Jones, the last entry mentioning Margaret was dated January 2000. A detailed 'digital investigation' of Cairney and Jones' mobile phones was also undertaken (in total, forensic specialists examined 594 calls and texts) but none showed any recent communication between Margaret and her carers.

Significantly, Cairney and Jones were not able to give the police any forensic profile of Margaret. The random items that Avril Jones gave to the police – a blue t-shirt, a tartan jumper, socks and a toy penguin – had no DNA traces of Margaret on them. Fortunately, the police managed to obtain a blood sample from Margaret's birth that had been kept by the hospital. The DNA profile extracted from this was compared against a number of unidentified bodies and body parts discovered across the UK. None of these matched Margaret Fleming's DNA profile.

Parts of the cottage, described as 'vomit-inducing' by investigators, were also demolished in order to search for any human remains.

The police investigation team at 'Seacroft' (led by senior investigating officer Detective Supt. Paul Livingstone) spent six months digging up the garden of the riverside property. The garden area at 'Seacroft' is extensive (over half a hectare) and so police diggers had to be brought in to lift up small sections of grass. Soil samples were then taken from these and sent for DNA analysis. In a move believed to be a first for Police Scotland, a mobile laboratory was set up in the garden so that items could be processed and prioritised more quickly. The soil tests taken from the garden were used to establish whether there were (or had been) human remains in the grounds of the property. Interestingly, 298 small fragments of bone were found in the garden at 'Seacroft'. However, they could not be identified as either animal or human because they were either too small or burnt to be treated as viable samples.

In addition to searches of the house and garden, police helicopters and dive teams were also deployed to conduct searches across all of the Inverclyde area. Due to the fact that the garden at 'Seacroft' runs directly down into the River Clyde, police divers were used to conduct a detailed search of the shoreline.

During these searches Cairney in particular continued to be mocking and critical of the police. Pointing to paving slabs at the front door, he said:

"They've not touched that bit. How could she not be buried under there? If you're going to dig a garden to look for a body, you've got to dig every inch. They had divers but the tide goes out nearly a quarter of a mile here. They were splashing about in 10 feet of water looking for a body..."

Was Edward Cairney, a retired diver and a man who had in the past owned a diving company, inadvertently

The police investigation of the garden at 'Seacroft' was extensive and involved diggers digging up the entire half a hectare garden in order to look for evidence: Credit the Greenock Telegraph

A mobile Police Scotland van outside 'Seacroft':
Credit the Greenock Telegraph

Forensic investigators taking soil samples from the grounds at 'Seacroft': Credit the Greenock Telegraph

The garden at 'Seacroft' after it had been completely cleared by Police Scotland investigators: Credit the Greenock Telegraph

IN THE CARE OF EVIL

Police inserted a fence around the property to prevent onlookers viewing the house from the main road: Credit the Greenock Telegraph

Detective Chief Inspector Paul Livingstone was the main Investigating Officer in the Margaret Fleming case: Credit the Greenock Telegraph

Forensic investigators carrying out soil tests at 'Seacroft' to look for any evidence of human remains: Credit PA

giving police clues about where Margaret's body had been deposited?

The painstaking search of the inside and outside of 'Seacroft' throughout late 2016, into 2017, in addition to the large number of witness statements collected, extensive 'signs of life' inquiries, and technical analysis of telephone calls, texts and messages seemed to be pointing to one conclusion. Namely that it was unlikely that Margaret Fleming was still alive and that Cairney and Jones, as the only people to have allegedly seen her recently, were highly likely to have had something to do with that. The police, however, still had no body. How would this affect their investigation and securing a conviction against the couple?

Chapter 4

No Body: No Case? The Police Investigation Intensifies

A key problem facing the investigation team was how strong the case against Cairney and Jones would be in the absence of Margaret's body. Despite ongoing searches of the property and the surrounding areas, no trace of Margaret had, or has, ever been discovered. From 1999 onwards there is simply no evidence of Margaret being alive. No one aside from her carers had seen her and she had not seen a doctor, used a bank account or been on social media in all of the passing years since then. With no body and no direct evidence that a crime had actually been committed, the prosecution was aware that the case against Cairney and Jones was a purely circumstantial one and could only be properly assessed once all of the evidence was considered in its entirety. However, circumstantial evidence can be powerful in murder cases, especially as it can help establish motive for an offence and questions around an accused individual's particular account of events surrounding a crime.

A common misconception in both Scots and English law is that a person cannot be convicted for murder in the absence of a body. While it is undoubtedly much more difficult for prosecutors to secure a conviction under these circumstances, it is by no means impossible. Securing the conviction without a body relies on the presence of strong circumstantial evidence instead. Circumstantial evidence is evidence that can lead to the inference that the defendant has committed the crime, to the exclusion of all other possibilities about what might have happened. In the case of Margaret Fleming this principle would lead to the conclusion that she was not missing but had been murdered, and that Cairney and Jones were the perpetrators.

Murder cases where there is no body are still extremely rare in Scottish courts, but prosecutors argue that technology has increased the likelihood of them being brought before a jury. For any jury, murder trials normally require two questions to be answered: was the death a crime and is the accused responsible? Clearly in cases where there is no body, jurors are also required to assess whether the alleged victim is even dead.

Under Scots law, crown prosecutors have successfully secured murder convictions without a body in a number of cases. In 2010 for example, David Gilroy was convicted of the murder of Suzanne Pilley, a bookkeeper from Edinburgh whose body has never been found. The prosecution's case was based on strong circumstantial evidence such as pictures of scratches on Gilroy's hands, which he had tried to cover up with makeup, and a voicemail message in which he pleaded with Suzanne to meet with him. DNA evidence was also found in the boot of Gilroy's car. He had also sent Ms Pilley 400 texts the month before she went missing, but these stopped abruptly after her disappearance.

Despite a huge police search operation, Suzanne's body has never been found. It is thought she was buried in a remote part of Argyll in a 'lonely grave' after it was discovered that Gilroy had driven to the same area the day after Ms Pilley went missing but had taken around two hours longer to reach there than the average journey. The prosecution's case against Gilroy, 49, was largely circumstantial but each part of it helped build a picture of his increasingly suspicious behaviour and pointed to his guilt. He was sentenced to life imprisonment with a recommended minimum period of 18 years in custody.

In the case of Arlene Fraser, there was also no body and no witnesses when she vanished without trace from the family home in Elgin, Moray, on the 28 April 1998. Her estranged husband, Nat Fraser, was found guilty of her murder after a second trial in 2012 despite Arlene's body having never been found. While Nat Fraser attempted to implicate one of his friends in the murder, he was convicted on the extensive circumstantial evidence against him. This included, amongst other things, suspicions cast on Fraser's story that his wife was alive but living somewhere else and the police discovery that he had tampered with items in the family home to try support his story.

Alex Prentice QC, prosecuting, told the jury the case against Fraser was circumstantial but that, from the evidence, it was 'quite an easy task' to conclude Mrs Fraser is dead. While Nat Fraser later appealed his conviction, it was upheld due to the strength of the circumstantial evidence against him.

In 2010, paedophiles Charles O'Neill and William Lauchlan were found guilty of murdering Allison McGarrigle in Largs, Ayrshire. Mrs McGarrigle went missing in June 1997, soon after she had threatened to report the men to the authorities for sexually abusing a young boy. The prosecution alleged that O'Neill and Lauchlan had murdered Allison in her bed and then dumped her body at sea. Her body has never been found.

While the prosecution's case was undoubtedly hampered by the lack of a body and the absence of any forensic evidence, it was supported by the evidence of numerous witnesses who testified that O'Neill had told them that Mrs McGarrigle was 'got rid of' and 'feeding the fishes' in the Firth of Clyde.

Both were found guilty of murdering Mrs McGarrigle after a four-week trial at Glasgow High Court. O'Neill was told that he must serve at least 30 years in prison while Lauchlan was sentenced to at least 26 years.

In the Margaret Fleming case, the circumstantial evidence against her two carers began to mount throughout 2017. While the evidence that police had gathered from the house as well as from vast external inquiries was painting a picture of Margaret as someone who had come to significant harm (rather than as someone who was missing), Cairney and Jones stuck to their narrative about what had happened to her. In addition to their story that Margaret was prone to running away from home, the couple came up with other scenarios to account for Margaret's absence. Avril Jones's mother, Florence Jones, told police that on 5 January 2000, her daughter had rung her up to let her know that Margaret had run off with a group of travellers. This particular tale of Margaret running off with travellers seems to have been a popular one that Cairney spun out to those who would listen. He used it when police first visited 'Seacroft' in October 2016. When asked how Margaret could have possibly left the house that night unnoticed by the dozen police officers surrounding the house, he reverted back to the 'traveller' story:

"Earlier we were on the bus she saw a traveller crony on the pavement. She'd have lifted her phone, phoned him and he'd have picked her up minutes after leaving here. I've been told since that is what happened."

When asked how he knew this is what had happened that night, Cairney could provide no explanation.

Such stories, no doubt well rehearsed between Cairney and Jones, were clearly designed to buy the couple more time to refine their story and importantly, ensure that they were both telling the *same* story to the authorities. However, their decision to go on and speak to the national media about Margaret was a spectacular misjudgement on their part.

In October 2017, Cairney and Jones agreed to do an interview with BBC journalist Suzanne Allan. This interview, broadcast on BBC television, ultimately sealed their fate because of some of the completely outlandish and fantastical claims made by Cairney about what Margaret was doing. It was also a revealing interview in that Cairney in particular came across as rather affronted and aggrieved that the police were even considering him and Avril Jones as suspects.

As expected, Cairney did most of the talking throughout the interview while Avril Jones remained quiet and largely unresponsive. Significantly, when asked by the BBC reporter where Margaret was, Cairney defiantly replied that she was alive but was living a nomadic life with travellers around England/Europe, often changing her appearance and name. Having spent part of his own childhood in Wisbech (Cambridgeshire), Cairney alleged that he had introduced Margaret to travellers and agricultural workers in the area. Cairney then went on to claim that Margaret was now a 'gangmaster' in Cambridgeshire, responsible for recruiting agricultural workers to the area. He went on:

"She stayed with a woman in Wisbech on and off over a period of years. She then became a 'gangmaster' who provided labour to farmers. She was bringing in workers from Poland. How she travelled without a passport I have no idea. She stayed there with a woman, Margaret Coe. That's where she went to begin with and she stayed there on and off over a period of years. Margaret Coe moved and I know where her house is but I don't know the address in Wisbech."

In the same interview Cairney cruelly ridiculed Margaret's disabilities calling her 'backward' and 'dolly dimple' (rhyming slang for 'simple').

IN THE CARE OF EVIL

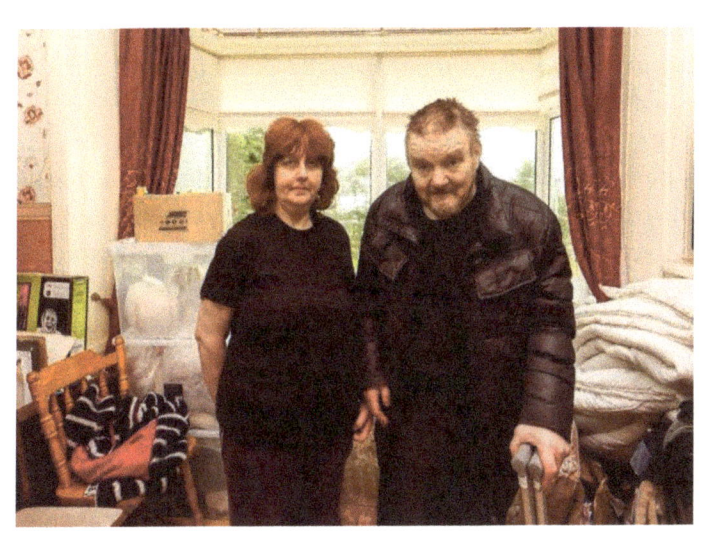

Avril Jones and Edward Cairney pictured together in their living room after giving several media interviews: Credit the Greenock Telegraph

As well as her secret life as a pan-European 'gangmaster', Cairney also alleged that Margaret was dealing drugs, stating:

"She's up to things now that I don't agree with and she won't be back here. Margaret is avoiding us, she's not missing. I know what she's up to, not taking drugs, but selling them and buying them. I told the police officer where there was going to be half a tonne of cocaine. I'm ashamed of this because I didn't really ever want her to be caught. She will get the jail. She will get caught. It's extremely sad that's what it takes. She's become a frustrated spy."

When Cairney was pressed to provide more hard information about the names and addresses of anyone who could corroborate these claims, he simply resorted to obfuscation.

Edward Cairney's claims in this interview – about a young woman with a reading age of eight, unable to look after herself or manage her own finances – were clearly nothing but ridiculous, absurd lies. The saddest part came at the end of the interview when the reporter asked Avril Jones what she would say to Margaret Fleming if she were watching the interview. Rather revealingly, Jones gulped, looked highly uncomfortable, put her head down and said absolutely nothing. Her silence seemed to speak volumes for the case against her.

The BBC interview with Suzanne Allan proved to be the couple's undoing. Within weeks of the interview being broadcast, Edward Cairney and Avril Jones were arrested by the police. They were arrested at Glasgow Central Railway Station as they were about to 'flee' on a night train to London carrying £3,500 in cash and the key to a safety deposit box in London.

On 28 October 2017 the pair appeared in private at Greenock Sheriff Court and each faced four separate charges. Crown prosecutors claimed that, between 1 November 1997 and 5 January 2000, they both abducted Margaret and locked her in a room within the property, where she was then held against her will. While held captive, it is alleged that they assaulted her, cut her hair, seized hold of her and then bound her arms and wrists with tape.

A second charge libelled against Cairney and Jones was that, between 18 December 1999 and 5 January 2000 while acting together, by inflicting blunt force trauma on Margaret or other means presently unknown, they did murder her.

Prosecutors also claim that the duo, having assaulted and murdered Margaret, and being conscious of their guilt, did then dispose of, destroy or conceal her remains. The charge further states that the couple then pretended to officials of the Department for Work and Pensions, social workers and officers from Police Scotland that Margaret was alive, and did this with intent to defeat the ends of justice; all between 18 December 1999 and 28 October 2016

A final charge alleged that between 18 December 1999 and 28 October 2016, when the police investigation into her disappearance began, Cairney and Jones pretended to the Department for Work and Pensions officials that Margaret was still alive and living with them to collect state benefit payments and claim Disability Living Allowance, Income Support, Employment Support and Carer's Allowance on her behalf while knowing she was dead, thus receiving £182,000 through fraud'.

The net was clearly closing in on the couple, their arrest coming almost one year after the police investigation at 'Seacroft' had begun. The circumstantial case against them was a strong one but in the absence of Margaret's body how would the case stand up in court in front of a jury?

Chapter 5

The Net Closes In: The Case Goes to Trial at Glasgow High Court

Following Cairney and Jones' arrest in October 2017, the onus was now on the Crown Prosecution Service in Scotland to prove their case against them. In law, it was not the role of the accused couple to prove that they were innocent or even that Margaret Fleming was still alive. Instead, the burden of responsibility rested on the prosecution to prove beyond a reasonable doubt that Margaret Fleming was dead and that Cairney and Jones were guilty of murdering her. The evidence against the pair was extensive but without Margaret's body or any idea of the specific circumstances of her death, prosecutors knew that they had a difficult task ahead of them. On 25 April 2019 Cairney and Jones went on trial at the High Court in Glasgow in front of Lord Judge Matthews, accused of assaulting and murdering Ms Fleming and fraudulently claiming £182,000 in benefits by pretending that she was alive. Each of the accused retained a separate defence counsel – Thomas Ross QC for Edward Cairney and Ian Duguid QC for Avril Jones.

At the outset, the key to the prosecution's case was the careful crafting of a picture for the jury of a young woman who did not have the ability to look after herself and whose life had been ended several years before by the greed and evil actions of the two people charged with caring for her. Moreover, that those same people had set about covering up their crime for the last 17 years in order to continue claiming their victim's benefits money.

High Court prosecutor, Iain McSporran QC, set about his case for the prosecution eloquently and with due regard for the complexities of the case. Central to the prosecution's case that Margaret was dead, was the testimony of a range of witnesses to help support the Crown's case that: (1) Margaret Fleming did not have the capability to live independently (2) there was no evidence to show that she was still alive and (3) viewing all of the circumstantial evidence together, Cairney and Jones were the ones who murdered her.

Witnesses from Police Scotland (called first for the prosecution) confirmed that they had first visited 'Seacroft' on the basis of a call from a concerned social worker about a *'very unwell'* 36-year-old woman called Margaret Fleming residing at the property in Inverkip. Police also asserted that when they arrived at 'Seacroft', Margaret Fleming was not there. One officer who attended even spoke of her *'gut feeling'* that Margaret had not lived there for a very long time. None of her personal items were found in the house and the bed in her attic bedroom showed no signs of recent use and was soiled and without a mattress.

IN THE CARE OF EVIL

Edward Cairney, 77 arriving at Glasgow High Court where he was on trial for the murder of Margaret Fleming: Credit: PA

Police testimony also confirmed for the prosecution that of the 1,946 photographs seized from the house, only five featured Margaret Fleming and all were date stamped before 1999.

When questioned by Defence QC Thomas Ross, police witnesses disagreed that Margaret could have evaded the watchful eye of the 12 officers surrounding the house that night and then taken off somewhere from the local railway station. This was supported by CCTV footage that showed no sign of anyone fitting Margaret's description in the nearby town at that time.

Key to the prosecution's case against Cairney and Jones, were the thousands of witness statements taken by the police to support the fact that no one had seen Margaret in a considerable number of years. Extensive police 'proof of life' inquiries showed no activity from Margaret in almost 20 years. DS Karen Boyd of Police Scotland was responsible for carrying out these 'proof of life' inquiries. Questioned by Iain McSporran QC, DS Boyd stated that there are a number of agencies and organisations that you would normally expect someone who is alive to either require the services of or be registered with. Through her inquiries over 12 months DS Boyd confirmed that Margaret had *not* accessed the services of any NHS GP, hospital, or dental service. Neither was Margaret registered on any social service database in the UK.

Margaret Fleming's local GP, Dr James Farrell, also testified that he had not seen Margaret as a patient since late 1999. This was an undisputable fact recorded on Margaret's health records. For a young woman like

Margaret, with a number of health problems, to not have visited a doctor in nearly two decades was a significant indicator that all was not well. At trial, Dr Farrell also confirmed that he had received a letter from Job Centre Plus dated 28 March 2006 regarding Margaret Fleming. This letter was to inform him that an application for benefits had been made on Margaret's behalf and that the Benefits Agency would no longer require him to provide regular medical certification as they accepted that Margaret was 'unfit for work' due to being 'permanently incapacitated'. This letter highlighted to the jury the fact that despite not having visited her GP since 1999, benefits were still being claimed on Margaret's behalf in 2006.

A key witness called for the prosecution was Mrs Alison Nugent. Nugent considered herself a good friend of Avril Jones's for nearly 36 years. Over the years, both women had enjoyed a friendship together, going on regular shopping trips and enjoying other social events together.

However, when questioned by Prosecutor Iain McSporran QC about how she first learnt about Margaret Fleming, Nugent replied that she only knew about Margaret from the local newspaper in November 2016 when it was reported that a woman named Margaret Fleming was 'missing'. When Nugent later telephoned Avril to ask where Margaret lived, Avril Jones replied that Margaret lived with her and 'Eddie' at 'Seacroft'. Nugent was clearly shocked as Avril had never mentioned Margaret's existence to her before. Mrs Nugent then stopped all contact with Jones as she *'couldn't believe the story any more'*.

Mrs Nugent also expressed her disbelief that 'Eddie' and Avril could actually act as carers for another person, especially one who needed additional care. She said:

"They were in ill health and their house was falling apart around their ears. They didn't have the wherewithal to care for another person."

The fact that Jones had never mentioned Margaret Fleming to Alison Nugent, a close friend of 36 years, until there was a 'missing persons inquiry' into her disappearance, speaks volumes about what she and Edward Cairney were attempting to hide.

Jean McSherry also gave testimony to the High Court. She revealed to Prosecutor Iain McSporran QC that she had lost touch with Margaret when Cairney and Jones became her carers. In court she stated:

"When Eddie and Avril had her, I got told that Margaret didn't want to speak to me or see me. I should've gone to social workers to get them to investigate Eddie and Avril. I beat myself up for that. I could've done more."

Not all of the witnesses called by the prosecution were effective in bolstering the Crown's case that something sinister had happened to Margaret. Paul Neeson, for example, an ex-firefighter living in the Inverkip area, testified that on driving past 'Seacroft' some years ago, he had seen a large fire emanating from the garden.

Neeson stated in court that, as an ex-firefighter, he recognized the smell coming from the fire as *'burning flesh'*. This however, contradicted his initial statement to the police in which he described the smell as *'burning animal flesh but not human'*. Edward Cairney's defence counsel quickly picked up on this contradiction and criticized Neeson for apparently changing his evidence in court. Following Mr Neeson's evidence, Prosecutor Iain McSporran QC stated that he no longer relied on Neeson's new account of smelling burning human flesh and Lord Justice Matthews then instructed the jury to ignore that part of the evidence.

The 'bonfire' evidence was not a good start to the prosecution's case. Cairney himself later stated during his evidence that he *had* lit a bonfire in the garden but it was only used to burn old furniture and pianos that he used to renovate.

Throughout the High Court trial, defence counsel for Jones and Cairney did their best to discredit the testimony of the prosecution witnesses. They did this by repeating the idea that Margaret could have decided herself to go 'missing' and that there could be other reasons for her lack of inclusion in official records that simply did not involve murder.

The defence's case was undoubtedly disadvantaged from the outset because a lot of the information about the case was already in the public domain through the numerous interviews that Cairney and Jones had given the media in 2017, before the High Court trial. The information was already 'out there' coming from the mouths of the accused themselves. Why the couple chose to even give these, what turned out to be damning interviews, is unclear. Maybe in Cairney's warped mind, he thought it advantageous to get their story 'out there' first. Maybe they wanted to 'lay the ground' for any future police action against them. Maybe they simply felt 'in the clear' after an intense year of police activity. Maybe speaking to the media simply appealed to their egos. Who knows? Probably one will never know the real reasons why.

The jury at the High Court first heard extracts from an interview that Cairney and Jones gave to Russell Findlay of Scottish Television (STV) on 4 October 2017. Findlay had visited the couple at their ramshackle house in Inverkip in order to ask them questions about Margaret Fleming's whereabouts. Neither of the pair had been charged at this point. Reflecting on his interview, Findlay initially expressed his disbelief that the couple, let alone a young woman with learning difficulties, could possibly be living in such filth:

"Most rooms were crammed with clutter and junk; the surfaces grimy. Random items, including a wheelbarrow, littered the gloomy hallway. The kitchen appeared to have been unused for years. An outside wall of one room was missing – a blue tarpaulin doing nothing to stop the autumn chill permeating every damp, dark corner. The stairs were virtually impassable due to further piles of rubbish and missing floorboards. The couple and their dogs appeared to live in a single room, warmed by a small gas fire. What must once have been an enviable and handsome property was virtually uninhabitable."

Prosecutor Iain McSporran QC, along with Russell Findlay, took turns to read out sections of the transcripts of the (STV) interview in court. In the interview, Cairney repeated his claims that Margaret was alive but was a 'gangmaster' and international drug dealer travelling throughout Europe on a false passport, and using a number of aliases. As with most of the interviews they gave to the media, Cairney did most of the talking throughout. Avril Jones only interjected once in the interview with Russell Findlay to state that she had the 'right' to claim Margaret's social security benefits and that when Margaret returned home, she was given the money. Edward Cairney also ranted to Findlay that the whole police inquiry against them was 'Masonic-driven' conspiracy involving corrupt council officials, Freemasons, the police, Greenock property deals, and Inverclyde Council. Cairney also mocked the police, telling Findlay how he planned to sue them.

Russell Findlay later reflected on the interview, noting how cold both were when they talked about Margaret:

"Cairney's... storytelling became more ridiculous, more outlandish and at times offensive. He shows no warmth while talking about Margaret, deploying ugly terms such as 'lunacy', 'backward' and 'dolly dimple'"

The damning interview that Cairney and Jones gave Suzanne Allan of the BBC on 7 October 2017 was also played for the jury in court. Reporter Allan spoke to the pair on camera for more than 40 minutes at their home. Called as a witness for the prosecution, Allan gave an account in court of how the interview came about. In this interview, Cairney repeated many of the claims that he had made in his earlier interview with Russell Findlay – namely, that Margaret was a 'frustrated spy' and 'gangmaster' who travelled all across Europe to deal drugs and recruit agricultural workers.

Both of these interviews were strong pieces of evidence for the prosecution. All of Cairney's claims came across as ridiculous, outrageous lies – particularly as they related to a young women who was unable to look after herself and live independently.

The strength of the prosecution's case against Cairney and Jones was starting to mount and take shape. The testimony of Cairney himself (Jones chose not to speak in her defence) proved to be highly damning to the couple's version of events. Not only did it show how combative Cairney could be as an individual (at one point he resorted to calling the prosecution counsel *a clown* and was reprimanded by Judge Matthews) but it also showed his defence that Margaret was still alive could not stand up under scrutiny.

Key to laying doubt on Cairney's defence was the introduction by the prosecution of two letters allegedly sent by Margaret Fleming from London to Edward and Avril, dated January 2000. Cairney stated that January 2000 was the first time that Margaret had run away and not come back on the same day. The couple assumed that she had gone to visit the Millennium Dome because she had talked about it before but Cairney was not able to take her there himself. He told the court that while in

London looking for Margaret, he and Avril Jones took it in turns to watch out for her at the dome but that she had *'given us a body swerve'*.

Cairney said Avril Jones had shown him three typewritten letters afterwards, two of which were posted in West London and one in Dumfries and Galloway.

In the police search of 'Seacroft', the typed letters were found after Cairney had informed officers that the letters were in the house somewhere. One of the letters, dated 13 January 2000 and postmarked London, was alleged to be from Margaret and was typed on headed notepaper from the Regent Palace Hotel in Piccadilly. The relevance of the letter, from Cairney's perspective at least, was that it appeared to support his claim that Margaret often ran away from 'Seacroft' and that she must have been alive at the time the letter was written because she was the author of the letter. Cairney also claimed that for 16 years after this London trip, Margaret had returned to Inverkip *'dozens of times'* mainly to get money from them.

In court, Iain McSporran QC read out the letter, which was riddled with spelling and grammatical errors, to the jury. Prosecutor McSporran, however, had one more 'trick' up his sleeve. The QC revealed that at the same time as Margaret's letter from the Regent Palace Hotel was being written, he had evidence that Cairney and Jones were at the <u>same</u> hotel purportedly 'searching for Margaret' in London. To support this, McSporran showed the court a sales receipt from the <u>same</u> hotel under the name of 'Jones' as proof that the couple had stayed in the hotel at the same time as Margaret allegedly wrote the letter. What were the chances that on the day that Cairney and Jones were at the Regent Palace Hotel in London, Margaret Fleming was at the exact same hotel typing a letter to them?

The sales receipt from the Regent Palace Hotel was a key piece of evidence for the prosecution's case because it pointed to Cairney and Jones having travelled to London themselves in January 2000. During their trip, they then wrote and posted three letters to their home that they claimed were written by Margaret. One of these letters was penned at the Regent Palace Hotel. The reason for doing this? – to create an elaborate cover story and false chain of evidence to suggest that Margaret was still alive after they had already killed her in December 1999 or early January 2000. What is unknown to anyone other than Cairney and Jones, however, is exactly how Margaret's life was taken and where her body was disposed of.

Evidence was also presented in court to support the Crown's assumption that Margaret Fleming simply could not have composed such a letter. Jacqueline Cahill, Margaret's former English teacher who was given the letter by police to look at prior to the trial, confirmed that:

"Margaret had literacy difficulties. She struggled to put pen to paper. She struggled to read, and did so at about the level of an eight-year-old...There are a lot of strange

spelling errors... A number of difficult words in the letters are correctly spelt and there is a stream of consciousness in the writing. Margaret could have written 100 words with short sentences and one idea. I would be doubtful about Margaret using a phrase like 'stopped in your tracks'."

Pointedly, Ms Cahill concluded that:

"This is not a letter that Margaret would be capable of writing."

In the witness box, Cairney could offer little defence of the letter or anything else. He continued to insist that he had 'dozens' of contact with Margaret over the years since then but had not seen her since late 2017. Cairney was adamant that there were people all over England who had seen her but would not come forward. He could not identify who these people were.

Cairney even claimed that shortly before he and Avril were charged with murder (in October 2017), he had seen Margaret in Tottenham Court Road in London and that she had been in a local 'Starbucks' coffee shop. Police examined all of the CCTV images from Tottenham Court Road from the 16 October onwards and found no evidence of Margaret. The only footage that police found was of Edward Cairney walking *alone* along Tottenham Court Road.

When Prosecutor McSporran highlighted such inconsistencies in Cairney's story, the 77-year-old lost control and began ranting:

"I can't sit here and let you put words into my mouth. I know my life depends on it. There is nothing sinister in anything we've done. She was a wee mixed up girl that we improved."

Despite Cairney's claim in court that he was *'incapable of harming a kid or a lady. I can't do that'*, he simply could not offer any concrete proof that Margaret was still alive. In the face of the prosecution's questions, Cairney became angry and biligerent, claiming that the police did not actually want to find Margaret. When asked why not by Iain McSporran QC, Cairney replied *"So as they can put me inside for life!"*

In Cairney's eyes, the whole crux of the Crown's case against him was simply to frame him and put him in prison. For him, the claim that Margaret Fleming had not been seen since 1999 was utter nonsense. During the High Court trial, Cairney seemed to believe that if he kept repeating his mantra often enough, that *'Margaret Fleming is still alive and we did nothing sinister to her'*, the jury would have no other choice but to believe him.

When questioned about the punishments that he imposed on Margaret, Cairney freely admitted that he regularly bound Margaret's arms in duct tape, wrapped them in cardboard tubes and also put a 'diving under suit' on her. However, Cairney claimed that these actions were motivated by good intentions in order to stop Margaret 'self-harming' and ripping out 'tufts' of hair from her head.

Towards the end of his questioning, Iain McSporran QC looked directly at Edward Cairney, forcefully presenting to him his opinion of when Margaret died and the couple's motive for killing her. This was a dramatic point in the court proceedings and is worth repeating here in full:

"Margaret Fleming was already dead before Christmas Day of 1999 wasn't she? You killed her Mr Cairney and you have spent the years since then telling lie after lie, cashing her benefits and living off Margaret...The reason you lied is because you had to cover up the most dreadful crime of murder."

Iain McSporran QC ended the Crown's case as eloquently as he had begun it. During his summing up he directed his final comments to the jury:

"I seek to persuade you ladies and gentlemen, based solely on the evidence you have heard, that Avril Jones and Edward Cairney bear joint responsibility for the murder of Margaret Fleming, a young girl with significant difficulties who had joined their household following the death of her father. Now, if the truth of the matter is that Margaret Fleming is alive and well and coming back and forth to Scotland as Mr Cairney claims, it would be surprising if she was unaware that the police were looking for her. It would also be surprising if she was unaware that Cairney and Jones have ended up being charged with her murder and it would be surprising if she didn't, in all those circumstances, think to get in touch on the phone to someone... Silence... As silent as the grave."

Prosecutor McSporran's closing remarks to the jury were as profoundly powerful as they were sad. His remarks highlighted the short, miserable life of a young woman who was simply forgotten by the system and ultimately killed by the two people her father had thought of as 'friends'.

As expected, the Defense QC's argued the Crown had *not* proven beyond a reasonable doubt that Margaret Fleming was in fact dead. Earlier the jury was told that Ms Fleming *'could turn up alive next week'* and that this was a case involving no body, no weapon, no crime scene, and no evidence of a violent confrontation.

Thomas Ross QC, for Cairney, said:

"You were invited to convict Edward Cairney of the murder of a person who could turn up alive next week, or next month, or next year. The advocate depute has invited you to convict Edward Cairney of the murder of a person whose remains could be found in a squat in Newcastle or upon a riverbed near Manchester next week, or next month, or next year, in circumstances consistent with a recent accidental death."

Ian Duguid QC, representing Avril Jones, told the jury they should not be blinded by prejudice or sympathy for anyone in the case and should not become involved in speculation or guess work. He said:

"My submission is you're being asked to do a lot of guessing if you're going to convict Avril Jones of murder."

Mr Duguid QC said the essential consideration for the jury is whether Ms Fleming is dead.

The QC went on:

"This is a case where there is no body. This is a case where there is no crime scene, a case where there is no evidence of a violent confrontation. There is no evidence of a murder weapon. There is no evidence of how she died, there is no evidence at whose hands she died."

He added:

"In my submission to you, the prosecution has fallen some distance short in trying to establish that this lady, Avril Jones, is a murderer."

However, it was the opinion of the jury that mattered now. After a trial lasting seven weeks, the 15 men and women of the jury retired to give their verdict. It took only three hours over two days to reach its majority verdict.

The jury found Edward Cairney (77) and Avril Jones (59) guilty of murder and guilty of fraudulently claiming £182,000 in benefits by pretending that Ms Fleming, who would now have been 39, was alive. The jurors supported the Crown's case that Cairney and Jones had murdered Margaret by unknown means between 18 December 1999 and 5 January 2000 at their home in Inverkip or elsewhere in Scotland and then tried to cover up the crime for over 17 years.

Lord Judge Matthews presiding told the pair:

"You have been convicted of the murder of Margaret Fleming. The only sentence the court can impose is one

of life imprisonment, however, as part of that I have to fix a period which must pass before you are eligible to apply for parole."

He deferred sentencing until 17 July 2019 pending reports. The pair showed no emotion as they were convicted of the callous crime. Cairney – who had been on bail– was taken down to the cells in his wheelchair. Avril Jones – who deliberately got herself remanded before the trial after calling police to admit she was breaking her own bail conditions – used her crutches to help her as she was led to the cells by guards.

Speaking after the conviction of the pair, Senior Investigating Officer Paul Livingstone gave a statement to the media. He argued that money was the main motivation of the 'evil and greedy' pair. He went on:

"The treatment which she was subjected to can only be described as horrific and the conditions she lived in were utterly disgusting and uninhabitable. For Cairney and Jones to continue the charade that she was still alive for all these years is abhorrent...We will never know just how Margaret was killed. What we do know is that she lived her last days in what can only be described as a living hell"

Immediately following the guilty verdict, Cairney and Jones were also served with a Proceeds of Crime notice. The Proceeds of Crime notice marks the intention of the Crown Office to recoup the £182,000 that the couple fraudulently claimed in state benefits over the 17 years that Margaret was missing. The sum being pursued

Detective Chief Inspector Paul Livingstone reading a statement to
the media following the conviction of Cairney and Jones:
Credit: the Greenock Telegraph

also included a four-figure cash sum found in Avril Jones's handbag as the couple attempted to board a late-night train to London from Glasgow Central Station just before their arrest on 27 October 2017. The sum further includes £25,000 that was found stored in a safety deposit box at the Metro Bank in London's Tottenham Court Road.

The Proceeds of Crime Act 2002 (POCA) typically considers not only the amount that criminals have obtained directly from their crime but also whether they have 'hidden assets' – in Cairney and Jones' case, the £25,000 hidden in their Metro Bank account.

In July 2019 Avril Jones's advocate John McElroy offered a partial payment on his client's behalf but the Crown Office rejected this offer in December 2019. A further court hearing regarding the matter is due to take place.

In 2017 Inverclyde Council served a demolition order on 'Seacroft' as the property was deemed 'unfit for human habitation'. In 2017 the property was purchased for £120,000 by two business partners from the west Midlands who had permission from the council to demolish the house. It is unknown how much from the sale of 'Seacroft' was sequestered by the Crown under the Proceeds of Crime Act.

Chapter 6

The Day of Judgement: Sentencing at the High Court

On 17 July 2019, Cairney and Jones returned once more to the High Court in Glasgow to be sentenced.

Lord Matthews sentenced the couple to life imprisonment and both were ordered to spend 14 years behind bars before they are eligible to apply for parole.

In his judgement Lord Matthews said of Margaret's murder:

"Precisely how that was accomplished and in what circumstances was not disclosed in the evidence and only you two know the truth. Furthermore, only you know where her remains are. As is disclosed in a victim statement which I have read, that of itself is, quite understandably, a source of immense grief as far as her mother is concerned. You were also convicted of covering up her death in various ways for almost 18 years. You were only caught after an investigation was prompted by extravagant information which you, Avril

Jones, provided in an application for benefits. It seems obvious that the motive for the murder and the ensuing cover up was financial. You, Avril Jones, were convicted of defrauding the State of £182,000 in benefits which you falsely claimed in respect of the deceased, although it was obvious on the evidence that you both had the use of that money.

"Margaret Fleming was a vulnerable young woman with evident difficulties. She was in your care and you breached the trust placed in you. The manner in which you spoke about her was cruel. The fantastic web of deceit that you spun was callous and calculating."

Lawyers for Cairney and Jones responded by saying that both maintained their innocence. Thomas Ross QC, representing Cairney, said:

"Mr Cairney continues to deny any involvement in the crime. He maintains that to his knowledge Margaret is still alive."

Ian Duguid QC, representing Avril Jones, said:

"She, like Mr Cairney, denies her complicity in any wrongdoing in relation to Ms Fleming. She, like Mr Cairney, maintains that the young lady remains alive or at least until 2017, when the last opportunity arose for them to have any contact."

The imposition of a life sentence by Lord Matthews on Edward Cairney and Avril Jones was befitting of the seriousness of the crime they had perpetuated. The pair effectively imprisoned Margaret Fleming for two years of her short life, kept her in filthy conditions, and treated her with utter contempt and distain. They ended her life simply because they wanted her money rather than the inconvenience of caring for her. The pair were entrusted by her father to look after her but instead saw Margaret as an easy solution to their money problems at 'Seacroft'.

Punishing the perpetrators of such a horrific crime is a fundamental part of our justice system and how as a society, we satisfy the ends of justice. Edward Cairney and Avril Jones, in the eyes of the law, needed to be punished for the horrendously evil act they had carried out.

The case of Margaret Fleming does much more however, than simply highlight the need of a society to satisfy the ends of justice. Crucially, it also raises serious questions about the ways in which at risk individuals, generally, are cared for and supervised in the community.

In Margaret's case, how was it possible for a clearly vulnerable young woman to drop off the radar without anyone in authority noticing that she was missing for 17 years? How was it possible for the actions of her two carers to go unchecked upon for so long? Why did no one in authority take notice of the fact that she was being mistreated by those very individuals who were not only claiming her social security benefits while she was alive but continued to do for so many years after they had already killed her?

These questions are clearly not easy questions to answer as they undoubtedly involve some apportioning of 'blame' and 'finger pointing' as to who or what agency failed in their duty of care to Margaret during her short life.

Undeniably, they are uncomfortable questions to both ask and seek answers to. Yet, they are necessary questions to answer if other vulnerable individuals like Margaret Fleming are to avoid suffering a similar fate to her.

In January 2020 Inverclyde Health and Social Care Partnership announced its plan to set up a Significant Case Review (SCR) of Margaret Fleming's disappearance. Led by Professor Jean MacLellan OBE, Director of Autism Network Scotland, the inquiry plans to investigate the role of all of the agencies involved with Ms Fleming, including Inverclyde Council Social Work Department and the Department of Work and Pensions. Prior to beginning the inquiry, a council spokesman stated that:

"This will be a full, independent inquiry which will involve all the agencies which were involved with Margaret during her life. A key area for the SCR team will be to uncover any lessons that are to be learned from the extensive cover-up carried out by Edward Cairney and Avril Jones to hide their appalling treatment of Margaret, while she was in their care, and the murder that they subsequently committed."

Professor MacLellan's report will be published once it is completed.

This Serious Case Review Inquiry is clearly a hugely welcome development and the hope must be that the findings of the inquiry will lead to fundamental improvements in social care practice and inter-agency working throughout the Inverclyde area, and in Scotland generally.

Chapter 7

Lessons Learnt and Caring for Vulnerable People: How Unique is the Margaret Fleming Case?

Sadly, the Margaret Fleming case is not unique. Over the last 20 years or so there have been several high-profile cases throughout the UK in which vulnerable children and young people have been killed at the hands of their carers. In 2000 for example, nine-year-old Victoria Climbie was killed by her great-aunt and her aunt's partner after months of ill-treatment and abuse. The young girl was burnt with cigarettes, beaten with bike chains, and tied up on a regular basis. Despite her numerous visits to hospital with dreadful injuries disguised as 'accidents' and warnings to social services from a relative, Victoria's aunt and her partner were permitted to keep 'caring' for the young girl. Social services failed to take appropriate action and Victoria's murder prompted the largest review of child protection services in the UK. The judge at their trial criticised the *'blinding incompetence'* of the people meant to protect her.

Similarly, in 2012 Daniel Pelka died at the hands of his mother and stepfather. For at least six months prior to his death, Daniel was beaten, tortured and starved. The Serious Case Review set up after his death found that Daniel was *'invisible'* and that *'no professional tried sufficiently hard enough'* to talk to him. The review stated that *'critical lessons must be translated into action'*.

There can be no doubt that during her short life, Margaret Fleming was also 'invisible' and was failed at a number of levels. First and foremost, she was undeniably failed by the evil actions of her tormentors Edward Cairney and Avril Jones. But she was also failed by the local social service department; failed by the Department of Work and Pensions; and failed by an entire social care system that could not seem to co-ordinate its actions in order to protect her.

In a rather obscure way, Cairney and Jones failed Margaret *less* than the others because their objective was always to abuse Margaret in order to gain money from her. Their standard was consistently low, motivated only by greed and evil intent. By comparison, the social care system might be seen as *more* culpable because its declared objective is higher and more worthy than despicable individuals like Cairney and Jones: that is, to manage 'risk' in society and in doing so, protect the most vulnerable.

During Cairney and Jones' High Court trial in 2019, witnesses from local authority agencies were called to give an account of their professional interactions with

Margaret Fleming. Their evidence was powerful but also highlighted the catastrophic consequences that can take place when services are either not coordinated or communication within agencies is ineffectual, breaks down or is not acted upon.

Evidence given at trial confirmed that a benefits investigator *had* indeed visited 'Seacroft' prior to Margaret being officially reported as a 'missing person' in October 2016. On the 18 June 2012, a benefits investigator from the Department of Work and Pensions had tried to visit Margaret at 'Seacroft' after she had not attended a medical check for Incapacity Benefit. During the trial, the investigator stated that she had spoken to Avril Jones (the person appointed by the Department of Work and Pensions to 'look after' Margaret's benefits) but was told that Margaret did not want to see her because of her 'mental health'. In court, the benefits investigator testified that:

"I reported this as a social work referral as I was concerned about Ms Fleming's and Ms Jones's living conditions and state of mind and also the fact that Ms Fleming was not registered with a GP. Ms Jones told me that it would not be a good idea getting a local GP. The living conditions were very, very poor. The house was really run down and not clean."

Prosecutor Iain McSporran QC asked her what she then expected to happen following her visit. She replied:

"A duty social worker should have visited them to follow up on welfare."

A social work team leader at Inverclyde Council then gave evidence as to why this follow up visit did not take place:

"We didn't get the client's consent and we basically closed it down as a referral."

A note written at the time, and shown to the jury at Glasgow High Court in 2019, stated that *'the referral did not ascertain the client's permission to make a referral and therefore no further action can be taken in relation to this.'*

The sad reality is that by the time a benefits investigator had visited Margaret in 2012, Margaret was already dead and had been so for a number of years. It seems astonishing that no further attempt was made to meet with Margaret face to face at 'Seacroft' to check up on how she was doing. Instead, social work and benefits staff relied on the word of Avril Jones to guide their decisions and did not apparently carry out any further follow-up meetings. *If* Margaret had been alive at this time, the dreadful sub-standard conditions clearly visible at 'Seacroft' should have, in themselves, merited further investigation. The fact that 'no further action' was taken because Margaret had apparently 'not consented' to see a social worker at this time, seems a shocking omission.

There are a number of lessons that could be taken from the above: (1) that missing any form of social care appointment *may be* an indicator of underlying problems with the child or young person at home (2) that in the event of a missed appointment, social care staff should then meet *face to face* with the child or young person in order to assess their well-being (3) that social care decisions should *not* be based solely on the word of a carer, especially when that carer states that the child or young person *'does not want to see them'* and (4) that any concerns about missed appointments, physical living conditions, possible abuse and neglect should *always* be followed up with a further face-to-face visit.

The principle of 'informed consent' is clearly an important one in social work practice. In simple terms it means that, depending on the particular circumstances of an individual 'client', a 'client' should, as far as possible, voluntarily consent to any social work interventions in the full knowledge of all of the reasons why these interventions are being carried out. Social workers have an ethical and legal responsibility to seek this consent prior to the delivery of all of their services.

While Margaret Fleming, if she was alive in 2012, would have been a 32-year-old adult woman, the reality is that Margaret could still not live independently and her learning difficulties would have made it very difficult for her to make autonomous decisions about her own welfare. The fact that social work staff defended their lack of intervention at this time, in circumstances that were clearly inadequate for a young woman to be living in, because they *'could not obtain the client's permission to act further'* seems unsatisfactory and unacceptable.

Even earlier than 2012, in the mid-1990s, there appears to have been oversights about Margaret's living arrangements. Margaret's social worker between 1995 and 1996, for example, stated in court that she initially met with Margaret once a week but this then became once a fortnight. In court, Prosecutor Iain McSporran QC asked the former social worker if she was aware that Margaret was staying with others (i.e. Cairney and Jones). She replied no.

In other words, following the death of her father and difficult relations with her mother, social workers were unaware that Margaret was living with Cairney and Jones at their run down house in Inverkip. This raises a key question. Namely, following her father's death in October 1995, were Cairney and Jones properly assessed by social services regarding their suitability in caring for Margaret? In 1995, Margaret was a vulnerable teenager with significant learning difficulties. She would have required support from individuals who were cognizant with her special needs. Given her difficulties, Margaret would have undoubtedly been a prime candidate for regular supervision in the community by official agencies.

In Scotland, as in the rest of the UK, there is a raft of legislation that exists to safeguard the interests of children and young people at risk of harm or neglect in the community. The Scottish Government is responsible for child protection in Scotland and within each local authority there is a Child Protection Committee that works with a range of local agencies (e.g. police, social services) to protect children. The Children and Young People (Scotland) Act 2014 sets out statutory guidance on safeguarding the rights of children and young people.

Safeguarding as a concept means protecting the health, well-being and human rights of adults at risk, enabling them to live safely, free from abuse and neglect. It is also about people and organisations working together to prevent and reduce the risk of abuse and neglect.

Safeguarding legislation, while clearly important, is only effective in so far as it is interpreted and *acted upon* by all agencies working in unison, ensuring that their collective actions are coordinated, double checked, realistic, proactive, and effective in guaranteeing a young person's safety.

Margaret Fleming undoubtedly 'got lost' within a social care system that had significant defective gaps within it. The dire situation that she was in prior to her death seems to have gone largely unnoticed. Sadly, the consequence of that for Margaret was that it made it much easier for Cairney and Jones to murder her, disguise what they had done, and then continue claiming her benefits.

Chapter 8

Discussion and Conclusions

Margaret Fleming's death at the hands of the two individuals charged with 'caring' for her, is a damning indictment of the system set up to care for vulnerable individuals.

It is clear that Margaret Fleming's father, Derek, entrusted Cairney and Jones with Margaret's care in the sincere hope that she would be looked after and supported by them. Sadly, this proved not to be the case. Cairney and Jones were in severe financial straits at 'Seacroft' and thousands of pounds in mortgage arrears. They saw Margaret as a way out of financial ruin. Margaret was shockingly let down at a number of levels. The fact that her murder lay undiscovered for 17 years is surely a poor reflection of how we operate as a society. For those long 17 years, no one in authority or from Margaret's family or friends, reported her as missing.

The murder of Margaret Fleming is also a tragic reflection of what can take place when a social care system is neglectful in its duty of care to the neediest in society.

One can only hope that following the Serious Case Review into Margaret's life, crucial lessons can be learnt and put into practice.

Nothing, however, should take away from the complete culpability of Edward Cairney and Avril Jones for Margaret Fleming's death. They, acting alone, took advantage of her vulnerabilities, ensuring that her young life was as miserable as it was short. For that, they have to bear full and complete responsibility.

Despite the numerous requests made to them by the police, Edward Cairney and Avril Jones have so far refused to reveal where they deposited Margaret's body. Police suspect that, given Cairney's experience as a diver, Margaret was buried at sea somewhere close to their old house on the Clyde Coast. The hope can only be that in the near future Cairney and Jones will find an ounce of compassion for Margaret's family, and reveal where her body is.

Lightning Source UK Ltd.
Milton Keynes UK
UKHW021000240720
367097UK00008B/122